Johanna M Marin

Laughing with Vampires

Table of content

Table of content...
Preface..
How to read it...
      The Standard Letters: ....
      Special Characters: ....
      Consonant and Vowel Combinations: ....
      The Dash ....
Romanian Idioms..
  "Who wakes up early in the morning, far reaches." ....
  "The neighbor's goat is fatter." ....
  "Who doesn't work, doesn't make mistakes." ....
  "To throw your boogers into the beans." ....
  "To shoot the painted crow." ....
  "To have a curly mind." ....
  "The dog dies from a long road and the fool from caring about others." ....
  "To pull on the right." ....
  "To hit the puddle with a stick." ....
  "To put your hand on the book." ....
  "To care for a snake at your bosom." ....
  "To put the saddle on dead horses." ....
  "To put your hand in the lion's mouth." ....
  "To cut leaves for dogs." ....
  "Whoever chases two rabbits catches none." ....
  "To have big ears." ....
  "To be like the devil in church." ....
  "To get impaled." ....
  "You met the devil." ....
  "To enter into bread." ....
  "To have the eyes of a vulture." ....
  "When the cat is not home, the mice dance on the table." ....
  "To have ants in your pants." ....
  "To get in like a fly in the milk." ....
  "Uncle Ion is getting involved too, because he's also a person." ....
  "Circles around like a fly to honey." ....
  "May the neighbor's goat die." ....
  "You went away as a cow, you came back as an ox." ....
  "To reconcile the goat with the cabbage." ....
  "Strike the iron while it's hot." ....
  "Damage in the mushrooms." ....
  "Who laughs last, laughs better." ....
  "Once upon a time, as in a fairytale." ....

"All bad leads to good." ... 30

"On the outside they present a painted fence; on the inside they have a painted leopard." 30

"He swallowed the dumpling." ... 31

"To beat the water in a jug." ... 32

"To hit the eye." ... 32

"To step on the light bulb." ... 33

"To do as your head cuts." ... 33

"The same Mary with a different hat." ... 34

"To disappear as if the earth swallowed you." ... 35

"To make a donkey out of a horse and a stallion out of a mosquito." ... 35

"To make sweet eyes at someone." ... 36

"To make someone with egg and vinegar." ... 36

"You don't inspect the teeth of a gift horse." ... 37

"The shirt is closer to the skin than the coat." ... 37

"What I had and what I lost!" ... 38

"What is born from a cat, eats mice." ... 38

"What you don't like, don't do to others." ... 39

"What's in the bird's crop is also in the tick." ... 39

"What's in the hand is not a lie." ... 40

"Don't give away the sparrow in your hand for the crow on the fence." ... 40

"What you do to yourself with your own hands is called manual labor." ... 41

"When two tell you that you're drunk, you should go to sleep." ... 41

"When two argue, the third wins." ... 42

"Who steals an egg today, tomorrow will steal an ox." ... 43

"The dogs bark, the bear moves along." ... 43

"That who distributes, gives the best part to themselves." ... 44

"If you excuse yourself, you accuse yourself." ... 44

"Nail drives out nail." ... 45

"With patience, you can even cross the sea." ... 45

"You chose until you picked." ... 46

"You have a book, you have a benefit." ... 46

"Have, give, don't have. Don't give, see how you have." ... 47

"To give it twisted." ... 47

"To give it like in Buzau." ... 48

"As you make your bed, so you sleep." ... 49

"Diligence is the mother of good luck." ... 49

"Who doesn't have an old relative, should buy one." ... 50

"If you've burned yourself with soup, now you'll blow even on the yogurt." ... 51

"If you sow wind, you reap storm." ... 51

"Who resembles, gathers." ... 52

"To put the cart before the oxen." ... 52

"Had you kept your mouth shut, you would have been taken for a philosopher." ... 53

"The fish starts to stink from the head." ... 53

"You're not going to make spring with one flower." ... 54

"Gift by gift makes paradise." ... 55

"Give to Caesar, what is Caesar's." ... 55

"After me, the storm!" ....

"After the war, many brave people come out of the woodwork." ....

"God protect me from my friends, because I will protect myself from my enemies." ....

"Beware of fools, because they have a rested mind." ....

"Become the devil's brother until you cross the bridge." ....

"Beware of the mute dog and the silent man." ....

"Hunger is the best cook." ....

"Brother, brother, but the cheese costs money." ....

"He who you don't let die, won't let you live." ....

"The old hen makes a good soup." ....

"The coat does not make the man." ....

"The uncaught thief is an honest merchant." ....

"Bad grass never dies." ....

"Ahead for pies, backwards for war." ....

"To the praised tree, don't go with the bag." ....

"At the poor man's, not even the oxen pull." ....

"The greedy one isn't satisfied, even if the Olt river flows through his mouth." ......

"Self-praise doesn't smell good." ....

"Laziness is a great lady, who doesn't have what to eat." ....

"The lazy one runs more and the cheap one loses more money." ....

"The work, once started, is half done." ....

"The wolf changes its fur, but not its habit." ....

"The gift is taken away from the dissatisfied one." ....

"Need teaches the man." ....

"The year doesn't bring what the hour does." ....

"There is no forest without dry twigs." ....

"No smoke comes out without fire." ....

"Tell me who your company is, so I can tell you who you are." ....

"The horses won't die when the dogs want them to." ....

"The left doesn't know what the right is doing." ....

"Not everything that flies can be eaten." ....

"Don't stick your nose where your pot is not boiling." ....

"Don't wish for it, because it will happen to you." ....

"The eyes are the mirror/window to the soul." ....

"Never trust green eyes." ....

"Brown eyes steal anyone's heart." ....

"Good watchfulness passes the bad danger." ....

"Until you hit your head on the upper threshold, you won't see the doorstep." ....

"To not be able to see the forest for the trees." ....

"Blood does not turn into water." ....

"The big fish eats the small fish." ....

"Don't leave for tomorrow what you can do today." ....

"Revenge is the fool's weapon." ....

"The juicy pear falls into the dummy's mouth." ....

"Be foolish, have luck." ....

"Put a bridle on your mouth and a lock on your heart." ....

"Don't trust the dog that wags its tail." 83

"Don't say 'hop' until you've jumped the pit." 83

"The appetite comes while eating." 84

"You recognize a friend when you're in need." 84

"Fools are not fools enough, if they don't also show off!" 85

"To be a gentleman or a lord is a random act; to be a human is a great thing." 85

"Let's stand crooked and judge straight." 86

"The well-fed doesn't believe the hungry." 86

"The wolf guarding the sheep." 87

"Even silence is an answer." 88

"The country is on fire and the old woman is combing her hair." 88

"The jug doesn't go to the water many times." 89

"Where you hit and where it cracks." 89

"Where the sun doesn't enter through the window, the doctor comes in through the door." . 90

"Last one saves the herd." 91

"One sick apple spoils a large pile of healthy apples." 92

"Long talk, man's poverty." 93

"Where there's no head, God help the legs." 94

"You speak of the wolf, and the wolf is at the door." 95

"A good day can be recognized by its morning." 95

"The house sparrow dreams of corn." 96

"Want it or not, Grigore, drink that holy water!" 96

"A lie has short legs." 97

"Haste ruins the job." 97

"Where there are many, the power grows." 98

"Eyes that don't see each other, forget they exist." 98

"You sell cucumbers to the gardener." 99

"The fool tailors it first, then takes measurements." 99

"Sweet talk brings a lot." 100

"Punctuality is the politeness of kings." 101

BONUS: "What would Romanians do?" 102

Preface

Ah, Romanian idioms – where language takes a playful detour from the scenic landscapes of Transylvania to th bustling streets of Bucharest.

Romanian isn't just about the horror of a blood-sucking vampire; it's a poetic language, packaged with a nation rich in folklore, traditions, wisdom, and humorous wit.

As one of the oldest languages still in use, Romanian has preserved the essence of diverse peoples: from the Asian-influenced tribes by the Black Sea to the Germani settlements in the Carpathians.

We inherited from them a linguistic repertoire filled with satire, kindness, cheekiness, and joy; a brilliant blend that can make you laugh or lose yourself in deep thoughts in a matter of minutes.

In the pages ahead, I invite you to laugh, ponder, and fall in love with the Romanian spirit.
So grab a glass of wine or a cup of tea, and celebrate the charm of this Latin exhibit.

Lost among the idioms?
In Romania, even getting lost is an exciting adventure.

And for those of you with Romanian descent, may this book be a bridge to your heritage; one filled with the vitality and resilience that only Romanians wear best.

Cu drag,
Johanna Marin

How to read it

While it shares many letters with the Latin alphabet,
Romanian has its unique sounds, marked by five special
characters.

Our comprehensive guide will begin with:

The Standard Letters:

- **A, a** - like 'ah' in 'father'
- **B, b** - like 'b' in 'boy'
- **C, c** - like 'c' in 'car'
- **D, d** - like 'd' in 'dog'
- **E, e** - like 'e' in 'bed'
- **F, f** - like 'f' in 'fish'
- **G, g** - like 'g' in 'goat'
- **H, h** - like 'h' in 'house'
- **I, i** - like 'ee' in 'see'
- **J, j** - like 'zh' in 'measure'
- **K, k** - like 'k' in 'kite'
- **L, l** - like 'l' in 'love'
- **M, m** - like 'm' in 'mouse'
- **N, n** - like 'n' in 'nose'
- **O, o** - like 'o' in 'pot'
- **P, p** - like 'p' in 'pen'
- **R, r** - rolled 'r' as in Spanish 'pero'
- **S, s** - like 's' in 'snake'
- **T, t** - like 't' in 'tap'
- **U, u** - like 'oo' in 'food'
- **V, v** - like 'v' in 'victory'
- **X, x** - like 'ks' in 'box'
- **Z, z** - like 'z' in 'zebra'

followed by...

Special Characters:

- **Ă, ă** - like 'uh' in 'huh'

- **Â, â** - similar to 'U' in 'Uber'; used in the middle of words
- **Î, î** - same as â, used at the beginning or end o words
- **Ș, ș** - like 'sh' in 'sheep'
- **Ț, ț** - like 'ts' in 'bits'

In addition to the standard and special letters in the Romanian alphabet, some combinations of letters have distinct sounds:

Consonant and Vowel Combinations:

- **Ge, ge** - like 'ge' in 'gesture'
- **Gi, gi** - like 'gi' in 'giant'
- **Ghe, ghe** - like 'ge' in 'get'
- **Ghi, ghi** - like 'gi' in 'give'
- **Che, che** - like 'ke' in 'kettle'
- **Chi, chi** - like 'ki' in 'kitten'
- **Ce, ce** - like 'che' in 'check'
- **Ci, ci** - like 'chi' in 'chin'

The Dash

In everyday Romanian speech, the dash often comes into play to form contractions.

The dash helps to bridge words, especially when two vowels meet. So its main purpose is to create a smoother flow in conversation, eliminating challenging pronunciation.

Examples:

Nu-i fac! (I'm not doing it)
Cine-i el? (Who is he?)
De-alungul (around)

The dash can be also used to distinguish prefixes or suffixes from the main word.

Examples:

ex-soț (ex-husband)

In certain cases, the dash connects two or more words to forge a compound noun. This link acts as a bridge, merging separate terms into a unified concept.

Examples:

franco-roman (french romanian)

In this book you will mostly come across the dash when in contractions. Don't get terrified. It actually works as the apostrophe in "it's"; plus it's made to simplify things; not to scare people away.

Romanian Idioms

"Cine se trezește de dimineață, departe
ajunge."

<u>*Word for word awkward translation:*</u>

"Who wakes up early in the morning, far reaches."

Meaning: "The early bird catches the worm."

"Capra vecinului e mai grasă."

"The neighbor's goat is
fatter."

Meaning: "The grass is
always greener on the
other side."

"Cine nu muncește, nu greșește."

Word for word awkward translation:

"Who doesn't work, doesn't make mistakes."

Meaning: "You can't make an omelet without breaking some eggs."

"A dat cu mucii în fasole

Word for word awkward translation:

"To throw your boogers into the beans."

Meaning:
To mess something up.

"A împușcat cioara vopsită."

Word for word awkward translation:

"To shoot the painted crow.

Meaning:
To fail miserably.

"Are mintea creață."

Word for word awkward translation:

"To have a curly mind."

Meaning:
Someone is cunning or devious.

My grandma would use this expression in another context, meaning: "Someone has a lot of intriguing and unusual ideas." (probably cause I was always up to no good)

"Câinele moare de drum lung și prostul de grija altuia."

Word for word awkward translation:

"The dog dies from a long road and the fool from caring about others."

Meaning:
Mind your business B****.

"A trage pe dreapta."

<u>*Word for word awkward translation:*</u>

"To pull on the right."

Meaning:
To take a break or rest.

"A dat cu bâta în baltă."

<u>*Word for word awkward translation:*</u>

"To hit the puddle with a stick."

Meaning:
Really fail at something. Also used in the context when you say something extremely inappropriate about a situation.

"A pus mâna pe carte."

Word for word awkward translation:

"To put your hand on the book."

Meaning: To really start studying or learning something.

"A crește un șarpe la sân."

Word for word awkward translation:

"To care for a snake at your bosom."

Meaning: Harbor and help someone who will eventually deceive you or become a threat to you.

"A pus șaua pe cai morți."

<u>*Word for word awkward translation:*</u>

"To put the saddle on dead horses."

Meaning:
To rely on something or someone unreliable.

"A băgat mâna în gura leului."

<u>*Word for word awkward translation:*</u>

"To put your hand in the lion's mouth."

Meaning: Someone taking big risk or acting courageously.

"A tăiat frunze la câini."

Word for word awkward translation:

"To cut leaves for dogs."

Meaning: Wasting time on useless activities.

"Cine aleargă după doi iepuri nu prinde niciunul."

Word for word awkward translation:

"Whoever chases two rabbits catches none."

Meaning:
If you try to do two things at once, you'll succeed in neither.

"Are urechile mari."

*Word for word awkward
translation:*

"To have big ears."

Meaning:
Someone is
eavesdropping.

**"E ca dracul în
biserică."**

*Word for word awkward
translation:*

"To be like the devil
church."

Meaning:
Feels very uncomfortab
and out of place.

"A luat țeapă."

Word for word awkward translation:

"To get impaled."

Meaning:
To be deceived or tricked.

"A dat de dracu."

Word for word awkward translation:

"You met the devil."

Meaning:
To get into big trouble. Also, depending on the context, it could mean to meet your match.

"A intrat în pâine."

_Word for word awkward
translation:_

"To enter into bread."

Meaning:
To really start working
seriously and hard
towards a goal; no more
fooling around.

"Are ochi de vultur."

_Word for word awkward
translation:_

"To have the eyes of a
vulture."

Meaning:
To be very observant.

"Când pisica nu-i acasă, joacă șoarecii pe masă."

Word for word awkward translation:

"When the cat is not home, the mice dance on the table."

Meaning:

People will misbehave when there's no authority figure present.

**"Are furnici în
pantaloni."**

*Word for word awkward
translation:*

"To have ants in your
pants."

Meaning:
To be restless or
impatient.

**"Se bagă ca musca-n
lapte."**

*Word for word awkward
translation:*

"To get in like a fly i
the milk."

Meaning:
To insert yourself into
a situation where you
are not wanted or don't belong.

"Se bagă și nea Ion că și el e om."

<u>*Word for word awkward translation:*</u>

"Uncle Ion is getting involved too, because he's also a person."

Meaning:
Used when someone decides to get involved in a matter just for the sake of it, though their implication is not of importance.

"Dă târcoale ca musca la miere."

<u>*Word for word awkward translation:*</u>

"Circles around like a fly to honey."

Meaning:
Can't stay away from something attractive.

"Să moară capra vecinului."

Word for word awkwar translation:

"May the neighbor's go die."

Meaning:
To wish harm on someor out of jealousy.

"Te-ai dus vacă, te- întors bou."

Word for word awkwar translation:

"You went away as a cc you came back as an ox

Meaning: Referring to someone who went on a mission or task and returned worse off or more foolish than before.

"A împăca capra cu varza."

Word for word awkward translation:

"To reconcile the goat with the cabbage."

Meaning: Trying to resolve a conflict between two parties so that everybody's happy.

"Bate fierul cât e cald."

Word for word awkward translation:

"Strike the iron while it's hot."

Meaning:
Seize an opportunity whe[n] it arises.

"Pagubă în ciuperci."

Word for word awkward translation:

"Damage in the mushrooms."

Meaning:
Used to describe a loss that doesn't significantly affect the overall situation.

*Word for word awkward
translation:*

"Who laughs last,
laughs better."

Meaning:
The one with the final victory or ultimate say enjoys it the most, despite the setbacks suffered during the process.

*Word for word awkward
translation:*

"Once upon a time, as in a fairytale."

Meaning:
Referring to something that happened a long time ago and is very unlikely to happen again, often with a sense of nostalgia or irony.

"Tot răul spre bine."

Word for word awkward translation:

"All bad leads to good."

Meaning:
Every adversity can lead to a good outcome.
Similar to the English saying "Every cloud has a silver lining."

"Pe afară vopsit gardul înăuntru leopardul."

Word for word awkward translation:

"On the outside they present a painted fence; on the inside they have a painted leopard."

Meaning:
Appearances can be deceiving. Someone or something might look pleasant and attractive from the outside, but inside, the reality can be very different.

"A înghițit gălușca."

Word for word awkward translation:

"He swallowed the dumpling."

Meaning:
He fell for a trick.

"Bate apa în piuă."

*Word for word awkward
translation:*

"To beat the water in
jug."

Meaning:
To waste your time,
repeating the same
explanation without an
result. Also said about repeating a useless act.

"A bate la ochi"

*Word for word awkward
translation:*

"To hit the eye."

Meaning:
Something stands out,
very noticeable, or
draws attention.

"A călca pe bec."

Word for word awkward translation:

"To step on the light bulb."

Meaning:
To make a big mistake, often one that attracts attention or has significant consequences. Can also be used in the context of cheating on a partner or disappointing someone close.

"A face cum îl taie capul."

Word for word awkward translation:

"To do as your head cuts."

Meaning:
To act impulsively or do things your own way without analyzing first.

"Aceeași Mărie cu altă pălărie."

<u>*Word for word awkward translation:*</u>

"The same Mary with a different hat."

Meaning:
When something that appears different is
actually the same, similar to the English
expression "same old, same old" or "old wine i
a new bottle." Also used to refer to a person
who claims they changed, but actually didn't.

"A dispărut de parcă l-a înghițit pământul."

Word for word awkward translation:

"To disappear as if the earth swallowed you."

Meaning:
To have completely disappeared; similar to the English expression "vanished into thin air."

"A face din cal măgar și din țânțar armăsar."

Word for word awkward translation:

"To make a donkey out of a horse and a stallion out of a mosquito."

Meaning:
To overreact about something insignificant.

"A face ochi dulci cuiva."

Word for word awkward translation:

"To make sweet eyes at someone."

Meaning:
To look at someone with affection or romantic interest.

"A face pe cineva cu ou și cu oțet."

Word for word awkward translation:

"To make someone with egg and vinegar."

Meaning:
To berate someone. Depending on context, i could also refer to making fun of someone in a demeaning way.

"Calul de dar nu se caută la dinți."

Word for word awkward translation:

"You don't inspect the teeth of a gift horse."

Meaning:
You should not complain about something that is received as a gift or offered for free.

"Cămașa e mai aproape de piele decât sumanul/haina."

Word for word awkward translation:

"The shirt is closer to the skin than the coat."

Meaning:
One's own interests are more important than others', similar to the English saying "Charity begins at home."

"Ce-am avut și ce-am pierdut!"

*Word for word awkwar
translation:*

"What I had and what I lost!"

Meaning:
Nothing. There's no regret about a situati
and if things were to happen again, they could jus
as well do; who cares.

"Ce naște din pisică șoareci mănâncă."

*Word for word awkwar
translation:*

"What is born from a cat, eats mice."

Meaning:
"Like father, like son
implying that children
will likely follow in their parents' footsteps
and/or way of living and being (or all other
aspects of their behavior for that matter).

"Ce ție nu-ți place, altuia nu-i face."

Word for word awkward translation:

"What you don't like, don't do to others."

Meaning:
This is equivalent to the English Golden Rule "Do unto others as you would have them do unto you."

"Ce-i în gușă și-n căpușă."

Word for word awkward translation:

"What's in the bird's crop is also in the tick."

Meaning:
What's on someone's mind is also on their tongue: when they say what they think.

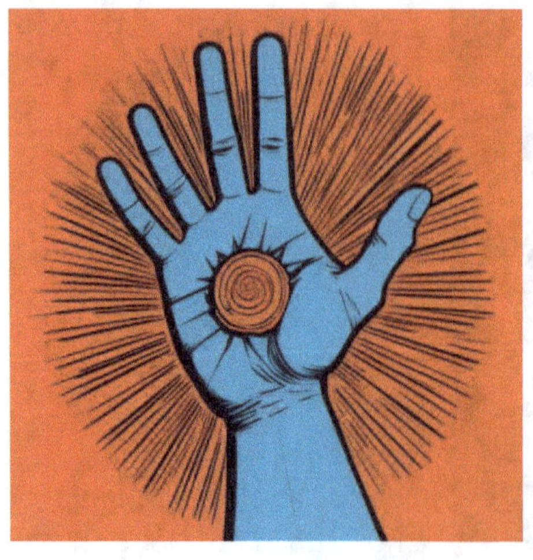

"Ce-i în mână nu-i minciună."

Word for word awkward translation:

"What's in the hand is not a lie."

Meaning:
A sure thing is better than a promised one which can turn out to be an illusion or potentially a lie.

"Nu da vrabia din mână pe cioara de pe gard."

Word for word awkward translation:

"Don't give away the sparrow in your hand for the crow on the fence."

Meaning:
A sure thing is better than a promised one which can turn out to be an illusion or potentially a lie. The equivalent of "bird in the hand is worth two in the bush".

"**Ce-și face omul singur cu mana lui se numește lucru manual.**"

Word for word awkward translation:

"What you do to yourself with your own hands is called manual labor."

Meaning:
Something a person does to themselves (by themselves) is of their own blame and they should now take responsibility for their actions.

"**Când doi îți spun că ești beat, du-te și te culcă.**"

Word for word awkward translation:

"When two tell you that you're drunk, you should go to sleep."

Meaning:
If multiple people are giving you the same feedback, it's probably true and you should heed their advice.

"Când doi se ceartă, al treilea câștigă."

Word for word awkward translation:

"When two argue, the third wins."

Meaning:

Similar to "When two dogs fight for a bone, a
third runs away with it," suggesting that when
two parties are in conflict, a third party can
often benefit from their disagreement.

**"Cine fură azi un ou,
mâine va fura un bou."**

*Word for word awkward
translation:*

"Who steals an egg today,
tomorrow will steal an ox."

Meaning:
Similar to the English saying "Give them an inch,
and they'll take a mile," suggesting that small
transgressions can lead to larger ones if left
unchecked.

**"Câinii latră, ursul
merge."**

*Word for word awkward
translation:*

"The dogs bark, the bear
moves along."

Meaning:
Ignore haters and carry on with your business;
similar to the English idiom "let the dogs bark".

"Cine împarte, parte își face."

Word for word awkward translation:

"That who distributes, gives the best part to themselves."

Meaning:
The person who divides something (like food, gifts, etc.) often gives themselves larger or better portion, akin to the English saying "He who cuts the cake must take the last piece."

"Cine se scuză, se acuză."

Word for word awkward translation:

"If you excuse yourself, you accuse yourself."

Meaning:
If you rush to provide unsolicited excuses, it's because you feel the guilt for what has transpired

"Cui pe cui scoate."

Word for word awkward translation:

"Nail drives out nail."

Meaning:
The best way to overcome or forget something is to replace it with something else very similar. Also used in the context of a competition, when only a very similar opponent can defeat the champion.

"Cu răbdarea treci și marea."

Word for word awkward translation:

"With patience, you can even cross the sea."

Meaning:
Patience is a virtue and it can overcome even the most difficult of obstacles.

"Ai ales pân-ai cules."

<u>*Word for word awkward
translation:*</u>

"You chose until you
picked."

Meaning:
You spent too much time
and overthought everythin
leading to your choice, thus making the wrong one.
Or in other words, putting too much effort into
making the right choice, you end up making the
wrong one.

"Ai carte, ai parte."

<u>*Word for word awkward
translation:*</u>

"You have a book, you hav
a benefit."

Meaning:
Knowledge and education
can lead to success or
wealth.

"Ai, dai, n-ai. Ia nu
da, să vezi cum ai."

*Word for word awkward
translation:*

"Have, give, don't have.
Don't give, see how you
have."

Meaning:
If you give, you may end
up without; if you don't,
you'll keep what you have.

"A dat-o cotită."

*Word for word awkward
translation:*

"To give it twisted."

Meaning:
To realize you made a mistake and now not know how
to deny what happened or find an excuse. Also used
when someone is trying to avoid a direct answer to
a question.

"A dat-o ca la Buzău."

<u>*Word for word awkward translation:*</u>

"To give it like in Buzau."

Meaning:
To change the subject or completely change your
attitude because you chickened out. Buzău is a tow
in Romania where the Carpathian Mountains make a
turn in a different direction (from a vertical
trajectory they have previously followed, they tak
an horizontal one). Hence, the metaphorical
representation of a twist.

"Cum îți așterni așa dormi."

Word for word awkward translation:

"As you make your bed, so you sleep."

Meaning:
The consequences you face are the result of your own actions, similar to the English idiom "As you sow, so shall you reap." or "You made your bed, now lie in it.".

"Sârguința e mama norocului."

Word for word awkward translation:

"Diligence is the mother of good luck."

Meaning:
Hard work and persistence often lead to good results, expressing a belief in the value of effort over reliance on chance or luck.

"Cine nu are un bătrân, să-și cumpere."

Word for word awkward translation:

"Who doesn't have an old relative, should buy one

Meaning:
The old relative represents the value of wisdom a
experience that comes with age; so yes, accordin
to Romanians, if you're not blessed with having a
old relative around you, you should look for one
Similar to the English saying "Experience is the
best teacher."

**"Cine se frige cu ciorba,
suflă și-n iaurt."**

*Word for word awkward
translation:*

"If you've burned yourself
with soup, now you'll blow
even on the yogurt."

Meaning:
A person who has been hurt or who has had some
unpleasant experience will be far more careful in
the future. Sometimes, overly skeptical and
suspicious of others. I guess "once bitten, twice
shy".

**"Cine seamănă vânt,
culege furtună."**

*Word for word awkward
translation:*

"If you sow wind, you reap
storm."

Meaning:
"You reap what you sow."

"Cine se aseamănă, se adună."

Word for word awkward translation:

"Who resembles, gathers.

Meaning:
"Birds of a feather floc
together."

"A pune carul înaintea boilor."

Word for word awkward translation:

"To put the cart before
the oxen."

Meaning:
Getting things out of
order or trying to do something before its time,
similar to the English idiom "putting the cart
before the horse."

"Dacă tăceai, filosof rămâneai."

Word for word awkward translation:

"Had you kept your mouth shut, you would have been taken for a philosopher."

Meaning:
Better stay silent and be thought wise, than to speak and remove all doubt.

"Peștele de la cap se- mpute."

Word for word awkward translation:

"The fish starts to stink from the head."

Meaning:
If the leadership in a group of people (like an organization, or a country) is corrupt, this will affect the whole society/organization. Responsible leadership is what matters most, right?

"Cu o floare nu se face primăvară."

<u>*Word for word awkward translation:*</u>

"You're not going to make spring with one flower."

Meaning:
Generally used to signify that one single good deed is not going to undo all the bad things you've done. Often referring to someone with a history of bad doings who expects to be seen/treated differently solely after one good deed.

"Dar din dar se face rai."

Word for word awkward translation:

"Gift by gift makes paradise."

Meaning:
Generosity and reciprocity create a better world.

"Dați cezarului, ce-i al cezarului."

Word for word awkward translation:

"Give to Caesar, what is Caesar's."

Meaning:
Everyone should get what they deserve. Used in the context of admitting someone was right in a certain situation despite not liking their character.

"După mine, potopul!"

Word for word awkward translation:

"After me, the storm!"

Meaning:
When a person creates a lot of havoc and then doesn't care about what they leave behind.

"După război mulți viteji se arată."

Word for word awkward translation:

"After the war, many brave people come out of the woodwork."

Meaning:
It's easy to act brave after the danger has passed. Used mostly as a response to those who like employing the annoying "should've, would've, could've" tactique.

"Ferește-mă Doamne, de prieteni, că de dușmani mă feresc singur."

Word for word awkward translation:

"God protect me from my friends, because I will protect myself from my enemies."

Meaning:
Sometimes those who are closest to us can hurt us more than our enemies.

"Ferește-te de proști, pentru că au mintea odihnită."

Word for word awkward translation:

"Beware of fools, because they have a rested mind."

Meaning:
Fools can come up with surprising actions and/or ideas as their minds are well rested.
Why? Because they don't use them. What can I say…
Romanian humor; don't take it personally.

**"Fă-te frate cu dracul
până treci puntea."**

*Word for word awkward
translation:*

"Become the devil's brother
until you cross the bridge."

Meaning:
Sometimes one has to make
alliances with less desirable individuals or
circumstances in order to overcome a difficult
situation.

**"Ferește-te de câinele
mut și de omul tăcut."**

*Word for word awkward
translation:*

"Beware of the mute dog
and the silent man."

Meaning:
Take this as a warning to
keep away from the people
around you who never give
their opinion on things. They can be unpredictable
or potentially dangerous given they keep their
intentions hidden.

"Foamea e cel mai bun bucătar."

Word for word awkward translation:

"Hunger is the best cook."

Meaning:
When you're hungry, even simple food can seem incredibly delicious.

"Frate, frate, dar brânza e pe bani."

Word for word awkward translation:

"Brother, brother, but the cheese costs money."

Meaning:
Even with close relationships, business and personal obligations should be kept separate. Often used in the context of a favor that a relative or close friend asks of you but you cannot make as it would cost you too much financially or emotionally

"Pe cine nu lași să moară, nu te lasă să trăiești."

Word for word awkward translation:

"He who you don't let die, won't let you live."

Meaning:

Sometimes, showing mercy to those who have wronged us may lead to more harm than good in the long run.

"Găina bătrână face ciorba bună."

"The old hen makes a good soup."

Meaning:

Experience, often associated with age, results in better outcomes. Sometimes also used to refer to the advantage of having by your side an older business or personal partner.

"Haina nu îl face pe om."

Word for word awkward translation:

"The coat does not make the man."

Meaning:
Appearances can be deceiving, and true value lies within a person, not in their outward appearance.

"Hoțul neprins e negustor cinstit."

Word for word awkward translation:

"The uncaught thief is an honest merchant."

Meaning:
Until someone is caught in a dishonorable situation or their wrongdoings are revealed, they may appear (and should be considered) honest.

"Iarba rea nu piere."

_Word for word awkward
translation:_

"Bad grass never dies."

Meaning:
People with bad habits or
intentions often seem to
persist, similar to the
English idiom "only the good die young."

**"La plăcinte înainte, la
război înapoi."**

_Word for word awkward
translation:_

"Ahead for pies, backwards
for war."

Meaning:
Some may be eager for pleasures but shy away from
difficult tasks or responsibilities; and those are
the ones that run ahead to get the pies but retrea
when war erupts.

"La pomul lăudat să nu te duci cu sacul."

<u>*Word for word awkward translation:*</u>

"To the praised tree, don't go with the bag."

Meaning:
Be cautious in regards to things/people/places that are highly praised or hyped. Don't set your expectations too high, as you might be disappointed.

"La omul sărac, nici boii nu trag."

<u>*Word for word awkward translation:*</u>

"At the poor man's, not even the oxen pull."

Meaning:
Usually when someone is down on their luck, even those things that should help them don't work.
Similar to "when it rains it pours."

"Lacomului nu-i ajunge, Oltu-n gură de i-ar curge."

Word for word awkward translation:

"The greedy one isn't satisfied, even if the Olt river flows through his mouth."

Meaning:

Meant as a critique to greedy people who no matter how much they might get, it will still not be enough.
The reference to the Olt river is metaphorical, because this is the longest river that flows exclusively within Romania's borders: from north to south passing through the following regions: Harghita, Covasna, Brașov, Sibiu (the domains of Vlad The Impaler and Bran Castle), Vâlcea, Olt, Teleorman.

"Lauda de sine nu miroase a bine."

Word for word awkward translation:

"Self-praise doesn't smell good."

Meaning:
Boasting about oneself is seen as unattractive or suspicious; that said, better keep it humble and show some humility.

"Lenea e cucoană mare, care n-are de mâncare."

Word for word awkward translation:

"Laziness is a great lady, who doesn't have what to eat."

Meaning:
Laziness can lead to difficulties in life, like hunger or lack of financial resources given it prevents people from working and providing for themselves.

"Leneșul mai mult aleargă și scumpul mai mult păgubește."

Word for word awkward translation:

"The lazy one runs more and the cheap one loses more money."

Meaning:

Those looking for shortcuts in life or a deal too good to be true without putting in the effort, will eventually end up working harder and losing more.

"Lucrul, odată început, e pe jumătate făcut."

Word for word awkward translation:

"The work, once started, is half done."

Meaning:

Take action and start tasks, as the biggest hurdle is often just getting started. Once you've begun, you're halfway to completion.

"Lupu-și schimbă părul, dar năravul ba."

Word for word awkward translation:

"The wolf changes its fur, but not its habit."

Meaning:

While people can change their outward appearances or behavior, their true nature or ingrained habits are hard to change. Similar to the English saying "A leopard can't change its spots."

"Nemulțumitului i se ia darul."

Word for word awkward translation:

"The gift is taken away from the dissatisfied one."

Meaning:
Those who are ungrateful or constantly dissatisfie risk losing what they have. It's a reminder to be more appreciative and live in the moment.

"Nevoia îl învață pe om."

Word for word awkward translation:

"Need teaches the man."

Meaning:
Necessity forces us to learn, adapt, and grow. Similar to the English saying "Necessity is the mother of invention".

"Nu aduce anul ce aduce ceasul."

Word for word awkward translation:

"The year doesn't bring what the hour does."

Meaning:
Sometimes, more can happen in a single moment than in an entire year. It emphasizes the unpredictability of life and the fact that significant changes or events can happen suddenly.

"Nu este pădure fără uscături."

Word for word awkward translation:

"There is no forest without dry twigs."

Meaning:
There are no perfect situations or groups; there will always be flaws, drawbacks, or less desirable elements. The same way that "roses have thorns".

"Nu iese fum fără foc."

Word for word awkward translation:

"No smoke comes out without fire."

Meaning:
Similar to the English saying "Where there's smoke, there's fire," it suggests that if there are rumors or signs of something, there is likely some truth or basis for it.

"Spune-mi cu cine te însoțești, ca să-ți spun cine ești."

Word for word awkward translation:

"Tell me who your company is, so I can tell you who you are."

Meaning:
The people you hang around with reflect who you are in terms of character, interest and beliefs.

"Nu mor caii când vor câinii."

Word for word awkward translation:

"The horses won't die when the dogs want them to."

Meaning:
Even though you've been through a lot, you will survive whether your enemies like it or not. Used in a satirical way in regards to the wishes of one's enemies when one is put to the hardest tests of life.

"Nu știe stânga ce face dreapta."

Word for word awkward translation:

"The left doesn't know what the right is doing."

Meaning:
A lack of coordination and communication can lead to people not knowing what happens around them. Used most often in reference to an organization where one department is unaware of the actions and plans of another.

"Nu tot ce zboară se mănâncă."

Word for word awkward translation:

"Not everything that flies can be eaten."

Meaning:
A warning that not all opportunities or attractive things are worthwhile. It's a caution to be discerning and not be easily swayed by appearances.

"Nu-ți băga nasul und nu-ți fierbe oala."

Word for word awkward translation:

"Don't stick your nose where your pot is not boiling."

Meaning:
"Mind your own business" and don't interfere in things that do not concern you.

"Nu-ți dori, că ți se va întâmpla."

Word for word awkward translation:

"Don't wish for it, because it will happen to you."

Meaning:
"Be careful what you wish for" cause it may come true.

"Ochii sunt oglinda/fereastra sufletului."

Word for word awkward translation:

"The eyes are the mirror/window to the soul."

Meaning:
A person's true color and character can be seen through their eyes; also used in the context of how someone's gaze can speak volumes about their intentions.

"Ochii verzi niciodată să nu-i crezi."

Word for word awkward translation:

"Never trust green eyes."

Meaning:
A playful warning based on a stereotype or cultural
belief that people with green eyes are untrustworthy o
mischievous. Most of the time, you'd hear this idiom in
connection to a romantic interest. Something within the
lines: "You know what they say: never trust green eyes.
Of course Romanians can't back this one up with any
scientific study.

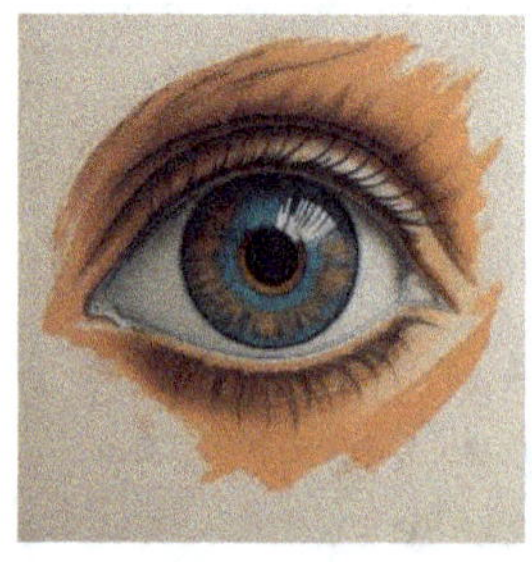

"Ochii căprui fură inima oricui."

Word for word awkward translation:

"Brown eyes steal anyone's heart."

Meaning:
Somewhere within the lines of the previous saying, this
one emphasizes the romantic allure of brown eyes.

"Paza bună trece primejdia rea."

Word for word awkward translation:

"Good watchfulness passes the bad danger."

Meaning:

Vigilance and caution can help avert danger or potential harm. Equivalent to the English saying "Better safe than sorry."

"Până ce nu dai cu capul de pragul de sus, nu-l vezi pe cel de jos."

Word for word awkward translation:

"Until you hit your head on the upper threshold, you won't see the doorstep."

Meaning:

Until you experience hardship or failure, you won't realize the good things you had in your life. Some Romanians can use it to refer to a significant setback that has to happen to recognize existing issues or challenges.

"Toamna se numără bobocii."

Word for word awkward translation:

"In autumn, the goslings are counted."

Meaning:
The results of your work are only clear after everything has been completed or the process is over. Similar to the English saying "Don't count your chickens before they're hatched."

"Nu vede pădurea de copaci."

Word for word awkward translation:

"To not be able to see the forest for the trees."

Meaning:
To be so focused on the details of a situation that you fail to see the bigger picture or the overall context.

"Sângele apă nu se face."

Word for word awkward translation:

"Blood does not turn into water."

Meaning:
Family bonds (symbolized by "blood") are strong and permanent, and can't be diluted or weakened (meaning can't turn into "water").

"Peștele mare mănâncă peștele mic."

Word for word awkward translation:

"The big fish eats the small fish."

Meaning:
The harsh reality of life is that the stronger or more powerful often take advantage of the weaker ones.

"Nu lăsa pe mâine ce poți face azi."

Word for word awkward translation:

"Don't leave for tomorrow what you can do today."

Meaning:
Be proactive and don't procrastinate.
Take action now rather than delaying the task for another day, whichever the task might be (private or professional).

"Răzbunarea e arma prostului."

Word for word awkward translation:

"Revenge is the fool's weapon."

Meaning:
Seeking revenge is a foolish act, suggesting that wise people would instead choose forgiveness.

"Pică pară mălăiață în gura lui Nătăfleață."

Word for word awkward translation:

"The juicy pear falls into the dummy's mouth."

Meaning:
Sometimes good things come easily to those who don't necessarily deserve a breakthrough. Also used to express you did all the work for someone else, just for them to reap the benefits. "Nătăfleață" is a derivative of the word "nătăfleț" which means dummy.

"Prost să fii, noroc să ai."

Word for word awkward translation:

"Be foolish, have luck."

Meaning:
It sarcastically points out that sometimes, it seems like luck favors the foolish or less competent.

"Pune-ți frâu la gură și lacăt la inimă."

Word for word awkward translation:

"Put a bridle on your mouth and a lock on your heart."

Meaning:
Discretion is probably best both in speech (saying less or nothing at all) and in revealing your feelings or intentions.

"Nu te încrede în câinele care dă din coadă."

Word for word awkward translation:

"Don't trust the dog that wags its tail."

Meaning:

Don't be too quick to trust those who appear friendly or cooperative. They may have alternative motives.

"Nu zice hop până n-ai sărit groapa."

Word for word awkward translation:

"Don't say 'hop' until you've jumped the pit."

Meaning:

Don't celebrate success prematurely or assume a task is done before it's truly finished. 'Hop' is an interjection Romanians use when they jump over a physical obstacle.

"Pofta vine mâncând."

Word for word awkward translation:

"The appetite comes while eating."

Meaning:
One's desire or interest often grows once they begin doing something. Even if at first a task or a person you hang out with might not seem fun or interesting enough to you, as time passes things prove to evolve exponentially better than you expected.

"Prietenul la nevoie se cunoaște."

Word for word awkward translation:

"You recognize a friend when you're in need."

Meaning:
"A friend in need is a friend indeed."

"Prostul nu e prost destul, dacă nu e și fudul!"

Word for word awkward translation:

"Fools are not fools enough, if they don't also show off!"

Meaning:
Ignorance combined with arrogance is the worst kind of foolishness.
Oftentimes applicable to someone who has definitely wronged but they don't want to admit their fault despite all evidence pointing clearly otherwise.

"Să fii domn e o întâmplare, să fii om e lucru mare."

Word for word awkward translation:

"To be a gentleman or a lord is a random act; to be a human is a great thing."

Meaning:
Nobility, humbleness, humanity and sympathy towards others are the most important traits you can build; having them is a big achievement whether you are a gentleman with higher social status, a lord or just someone on the street.

"Să stăm strâmb și să judecăm drept."

Word for word awkward translation:

"Let's stand crooked and judge straight."

Meaning:
We must be objective and fair in our judgment, despite our personal biases. Similar to when talking to a close friend you find yourself saying "between you and me, these are the facts whether we like it or not".

"Sătulul nu crede flămândului."

Word for word awkward translation:

"The well-fed doesn't believe the hungry."

Meaning:
It's hard for people in comfortable situations to understand the struggles of those in hardship.

"Lupul paznic la oi."

<u>*Word for word awkward translation:*</u>

"The wolf guarding the sheep."

Meaning:
When someone is given a role they: a) are completely unsuited for; b) did everything to get in order to exploit for their own benefit. Similar to the English saying "like a fox guarding the henhouse".

"Și tăcerea e un răspuns."

Word for word awkward translation:

"Even silence is an answer."

Meaning:
Not responding or staying silent can convey a message as effectively as words.

"Țara arde și baba se piaptănă."

Word for word awkward translation:

"The country is on fire and the old woman is combing her hair."

Meaning:
Ignoring major problems related to the bigger picture, while focusing on the less stressful, but less significant aspects.

"Ulciorul nu merge de multe ori la apă."

Word for word awkward translation:

"The jug doesn't go to the water many times."

Meaning:

Too much reliance on luck when you take risks can eventually lead to disaster. In other words, there is a limit to the amount of times you just get lucky without shedding a tear.

"Unde dai și unde crapă."

Word for word awkward translation:

"Where you hit and where it cracks."

Meaning:

Unexpected consequences can arise from our actions, sometimes in areas we didn't anticipate.

"Unde nu intră soarele pe fereastră, intră doctorul pe ușă."

Word for word awkward translation:

"Where the sun doesn't enter through the window, the doctor comes in throug the door."

Meaning:
A lack of sunlight and fresh air (or general neglect of health) can lea to illness.

"Urma scapă turma."

"Last one saves the herd."

Meaning:
The last one in the herd will be attacked and eaten,
thus saving the rest of the individuals. Looks like the
demise of the weakest link is not always a bad outcome
for the rest of the operation.
When I was growing up (I am a late 80's baby), we would
chant **"Urma scapă turma"** while playing hide-and-seek.
This was meant to signal to the final player still in
hiding that they are the last one standing. Now they
could plan their next move to tag the seeker and win the
whole game for all of us.

"Un măr bolnav strică o gramadă mare de mere sănătoase."

Word for word awkward translation:

"One sick apple spoils a large pile of healthy apples."

Meaning:
One bad influence can have a negative effect on the whole group. Similar to "one bad apple can spoil the bunch".

"Vorba lungă, sărăcia omului."

Word for word awkward translation:

"Long talk, man's poverty."

Meaning:
Talking too much, especially without action, is a sign of ineffectiveness or lack of substance.

"Unde nu-i cap, vai de picioare."

Word for word awkward translation:

"Where there's no head, God help the legs."

Meaning:
Without proper leadership or guidance, things can
quickly become chaotic and directionless. "Vai" is
one of those words impossible to translate; an
interjection Romanians use to express pain, terror
or shock in a very dramatic way. Sometimes too
overly dramatic. Examples: "Vai, ce mă doare capul
(what a headache!!!); "Vai, a zis asta?" (did he
really say that?);"Vai, nu se poate!" (It's
impossible!!! I can't believe it!)

"Vorbești de lup și lupul la ușă."

Word for word awkward translation:

"You speak of the wolf, and the wolf is at the door."

Meaning:
Similar to the English saying "Speak of the devil and he shall appear."

"Ziua bună se cunoaște de dimineață."

Word for word awkward translation:

"A good day can be recognized by its morning."

Meaning:
The way a situation begins, often indicates how it will continue or end. Similar to the English saying "Morning shows the day."

"Vrabia mălai visează."

*Word for word awkward
translation:*

"The house sparrow dreams of corn."

Meaning:
Every one of us can sit daydreaming about what we desire
or need the most.
Oftentimes used in a satirical way in regards to those
things we can't achieve, yet (at least) can dream of.
For the sake of humor, we will sometimes replace the
word **"mălai visează"** (which translates to "dreams of
corn") with **"Mihai Viteazul"** (Michael The Brave, Prince
of Moldavia). Don't ask me why…

"Vrei, nu vrei, bea, Grigore aghiasmă!"

*Word for word awkward
translation:*

"Want it or not, Grigore, drin
that holy water!"

Meaning:
Sometimes, one must do things they may not want to
for their own good. Grigore is a Romanian name wit
roots in another popular (more international) name
George.

"Minciuna are picioare scurte."

Word for word awkward translation:

"A lie has short legs."

Meaning:
Sooner or later the truth will come out and you won't be able to lie forever. Hence the short legs.

"Graba strică treaba."

Word for word awkward translation:

"Haste ruins the job."

Meaning:
Rushing to complete something will always lead to mistakes.

"Unde-s mulți, puterea crește."

Word for word awkward translation:

"Where there are many, the power grows."

Meaning:
There is strength in numbers.

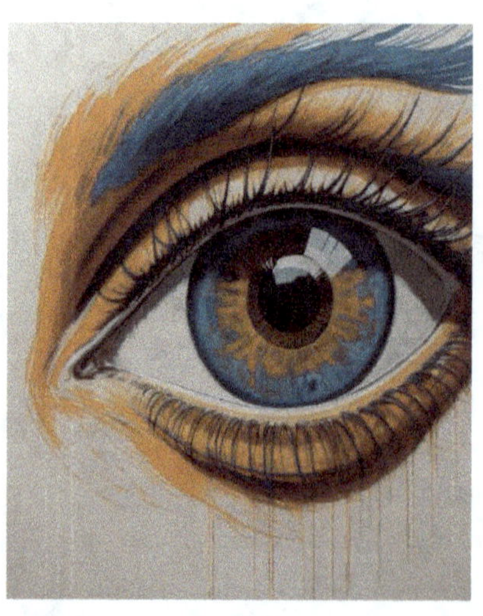

"Ochii care nu se văd, s uită."

Word for word awkward translation:

"Eyes that don't see each other, forget they exist."

Meaning:
Out of sight, out of mind. Distance and lack of contact might eventually lead to forgetting about a person. Used to refer to people who haven't seen/kept contact with each other for long periods of time and eventually cut ties.

"Vinzi castraveți grădinarului."

Word for word awkward translation:

"You sell cucumbers to the gardener."

Meaning:
Attempting to deceive or fool someone about something they already know well; also trying to teach an expert their own craft. Which is naive and cheeky to do, right?

"Prostul întâi o croiește apoi o gândește."

Word for word awkward translation:

"The fool tailors it first, then takes measurements."

Meaning:
Meant as a playful admonishment against acting before thinking or planning. Take this as a warning against hasty decisions or actions.

"Vorba dulce mult aduce."

<u>*Word for word awkward translation:*</u>

"Sweet talk brings a lot."

Meaning:
A kind, gentle, or persuasive way of approaching someone can often achieve more than a harsh or aggressive one. Similar to the English idiom "You catch more flies with honey than with vinegar."

"Punctualitatea este politețea regilor."

<u>*Word for word awkward translation:*</u>

"Punctuality is the politeness of kings."

Meaning:

The importance of being on time and the respect for others' time is here raised at the highest rank. So much so that it is compared to the politeness which only kings exhibit. A mark of good character after all.

BONUS: "What would Romanians do?"

100 short expressions that talk about the same things you surely experience every day by describing them in a very different way: the sparkling Romanian way.

Here comes the final chapter of this book entitled "What would Romanians do?"

Make it 100 and some change.

ENJOY!

1.   Romanians won't *"tell you to stop wasting time"*...
they'll say "don't rub the mint" .

Nu freca menta!

2.   Romanians aren't just *"lucky"*...
they are "kissed by fortune".

Sărutat de noroc.

3.   Romanians won't *"tell you to go away"*...
they'll tell you to "walk the bear".

Plimbă ursul!

4.   Romanians won't *"eat too much"*...
"the Turks will fight at their mouth".

Se bat turcii la gura lui.

5.   Romanians don't just *"miss an opportunity"*...
they "miss the cow with the hay" .

A rata vaca cu fânul.

6.   Romanians don't *"have many problems"*...
they "have the sky falling on their head" .

Îi cade cerul în cap.

7.   Romanians don't *"cause trouble to their enemy"*...
they "put sticks into their wheels" .

Pune bețe în roate.

8.   Romanians don't *"work hard"*...
they "break in pieces like a dog".

Se rupe ca un câine.

9.   Romanians aren't just *"stubborn"*...
they "bang their head against the wall".

Se dă cu capul de pereți.

10.   Romanians won't *"ask for too much"*...
they'll "want the sun and the moon from the sky".

Vrea soarele și luna de pe cer.

11.   Romanians don't just *"laugh"*...
they "laugh with their mouths all the way to their
ears".

Râde cu gura până la urechi.

12.   Romanians don't *"get angry easily"*...
they "catch fire like gunpowder".

Se aprinde ca praful de pușcă.

13.   Romanians don't *"fail completely"*...
    they "break like glass".

Se sparge ca sticla.

14.   Romanians won't *"talk nonsense"*...
    they'll "throw words into the wind".

Arună vorbe în vânt.

15.   Romanians won't *"be suspicious"*...
    they'll "smell a cooked thing".

Miroase a lucru gătit.

16.   Romanians won't *"reject an idea right away"*...
    they'll "not swallow it with bread".

Nu o înghite cu pâine.

17.   Romanians won't *"do something hastily"*...
    they'll "jump over stages".

Sare peste etape.

18.   Romanians won't *"lie to you"*...
    they'll "sell you doughnuts".

Vinde gogoși.

19.   Romanians won't *"try to fool you"*...
   they'll "throw dust in your eyes".

   Aruncă praf în ochi.

20.   Romanians won't *"make a mistake"*...
   they'll "step on the cheese grater".

   Calcă pe răzătoare.

21.   Romanians won't *"be confused"*...
   they'll "no longer know where their head is".

   Nu-și mai știe de cap.

22.   Romanians won't *"be very happy"*...
   they'll "jump on one foot".

   Sare într-un picior.

23.   Romanians won't *"refuse to deal with you"*...
they'll "send you to pick cherries".

Te trimite la cules de cireșe.

24.   Romanians won't *"be impatient"*...
they'll "burn with impatience".

Arde de nerăbdare.

25.   Romanians won't *"be curious"*...
they'll "burn with curiosity".

Arde de curiozitate.

26.   Romanians don't *"ignore you"*...
they "look through you like through glass".

Se uită prin tine ca prin geam.

27.   Romanians don't *"suddenly get it"*...
their "coin drops".

Îi pică fisa.

28.   Romanians don't just *"get bored"*...
they "die of boredom".

Moare de plictiseală.

29.   Romanians don't *"make a grand entrance"*...
they "come with trumpets and horns."

Vine cu surle si trâmbițe.

30.   Romanians won't just *"announce something important"*...
they'll "give you the news with the bell".

Îți dă vestea cu clopotul.

31.   You don't *"drive Romanians nuts"*...
you "take them out of their watermelons".

Îl scoți din pepeni.

32.   Romanians don't *"waste time in vain"*...
they "shoot their guns into the birds".

Trage cu pușca în rândunele.

33.   Romanians won't just *"annoy you with the same question on and on again"*...
"they'll beat you on the head".

Te bate la cap.

34.   Romanians won't just *"experience the imposter syndrome"*...
"they'll feel with the fly on their hat".

Se simte cu musca pe căciulă.

35.   Romanians won't just *"get upset"*...
"they'll boil in their own juice".

Fierbe în suc propriu.

36.   Romanians don't just *"help you"*...
"they'll give you a hand of help".

Îți dă o mână de ajutor.

37.   Romanians aren't just *"eccentric"*...
"they are gone with the raft".

Dus cu pluta.

38.   Romanians don't *"fool themselves"*...
"they get drunk on cold water".

Te îmbeți cu apă rece.

39.   Romanians wont *"wait for a long time"*...
"they will wait until the cows come home".

Așteaptă până vine vaca acasă.

40.   Romanians don't just *"lose patience"*...
"they will jump out of their character".

A sări din fire.

41.   Romanians won't just *"get angry"*...
"their mustard will jump off".

Îi sare muștarul.

42.   Something isn't just *"obvious"* to Romanians...
it "jumps in their eyes".

A sări în ochi.

43.   Romanians won't just *"be confused"*...
they will "not know what's with them".

A nu ști ce-i cu tine.

44.   To Romanians one is not just *"uneducated"*...
they are "a Venice bush".

Tufă de Veneția.

45.   Romanians won't just *"worry about something"*...
their problems "will eat at their liver" or "will ea
their days away".

A-ți mânca ficatul.

46.   Romanians won't simply call someone *"dishonest"*
 or *"untrustworthy"*...
 they'll refer to them as a "spotted horse".

Cal breaz.

47.   Romanians don't just *"do something pointless"*...
 they'll "rub ointment on a wooden leg" .

Frecție la picior de lemn.

48.   Romanians don't just *"become astonished"*...
 their "face will fall off" .

I-a picat fața.

49.   Romanians don't just *"barely escape"*...
 they "escape through the ears of the needle" .

Scapă ca prin urechile acului.

50.   Romanians don't just *"brave a situation"*...
 they "take their heart in their teeth" .

A-și lua inima în dinți.

51.   Romanians don't *"wait forever"*...
 they wait "until the horses' Easter" .

Așteaptă până la Paștele cailor.

52.   Romanians don't just *"wish you luck"*...
they "hold their fists for you" .

Îți țin pumnii.

53.   Romanians don't just say *"you're old"*...
they say "death is looking for you at home" .

Te caută moartea pe acasă.

54.   Romanians don't just *"daydream"*...
they "dream of green horses on the walls" .

Visează la cai verzi pe pereți.

55.   Romanians don't just *"look confused"*...
they "look like a calf at a new gate" .

A se uita ca vițelul la poarta nouă.

56.   Romanians don't just *"give up"*...
they "stick their feet in the situation" .

A-și băga picioarele.

57.   Romanians don't just *"deceive others"*...
they "walk around with a painted crow" .

A umbla cu cioara vopsită.

58.   Romanians don't just *"have a way to get to*
   somebody who's done them wrong"...
   they "have a needle for somebody's coat" .

Are ac de cojocul lui.

59.   Romanians don't just *"trust someone deeply"*...
   they "put their hand in the fire for someone" .

A băga mâna în foc pentru cineva.

60.   Romanians don't just *"deceive you"*...
   they "take you with the rug" .

A te duce cu preșul.

61.   Romanians don't just *"fight a losing battle"*...
   they "fight the windmills" .

Te lupți cu morile de vânt.

62.   Romanians don't just *"pass unaffected and unharmed*
   by a situation"...

   they "pass like a goose through water" .

A trece ca gâsca prin apă.

63.   Romanians aren't just *"nervous"*...
they "have a carrot up their ass" .

Are un morcov in fund.

64.   Romanians don't just *"surprise and amaze their
friends/inner circle with an achievement"*...
they "break the mouth of the market".

Rupe gura targului.

65.   To a Romanian you aren't just *"unlucky"*...
you "have a black cloud over your head".

Are un nor negru deasupra capului.

66.   Romanians don't just *"go to bed early"*...
they "go to bed with the chickens".

Se culcă odată cu găinile.

67.   Romanians don't just *"tell it like it is"*...
they "put the cards face up".

Pune cărțile pe față.

68.   Romanians don't just *"take a risk"*...
they "throw themselves head forward".

Se aruncă cu capul înainte.

69.   Romanians don't just *"act suspiciously"*...
they "have a tail".

Are coadă.

70.   Romanians don't just *"confront their problems"*...
they "take the bull by the horns".

Ia taurul de coarne.

71.   Romanians don't just *"give up"*...
they "throw the pen".

Aruncă condeiul.

72.   Romanians don't just *"fail to make sense of
something"*...
they "listen to you speaking Chinese".

Parcă îmi vorbești chinezește.

73.   Romanians don't just *"face a difficult situation"*...
they "are between the hammer and the anvil".

Între ciocan și nicovală.

74.   Romanians aren't just *"scared and shocked"*...
they "make crosses".

A face cruci.

75.   Romanians don't just *"behave arrogantly"*...
they "hold the nose up high".

Ține nasul pe sus.

76.   Romanians don't just *"get surprised and shocked"*...
they "remain as if struck by lightning".

Rămâne ca lovit de trăsnet.

77.   Romanians don't just *"get very tired"*...
they "fall off their feet".

Cade din picioare.

78.   Romanians don't just *"complain without cause"*...
they "howl at the moon".

Urlă la lună.

79.   Romanians don't just *"take you for granted"*...
they "have you at the little finger".

Te are la degetul mic.

80.   Romanians don't just *"look for trouble"*...
they "enter the wasp's nest".

Intră în cuibul viespilor.

81.   Romanians don't just "whisper *to you the right
answer at school"*...
they "blow it to you".

Îți suflă răspunsul.

82.   Romanians don't just *"beat around the bush"*...
they "spin around like the cat around its tail".

Se învârte ca pisica în jurul cozii.

83.   Romanians don't just *"lose their temper"*...
"their spark jumps out".

Îi sare scânteia.

84.   Romanians don't just *"stare blankly"*...
they "stare like a cat at the calendar".

A se uita ca mâta-n calendar.

85.   Romanians don't just *"mess something up"*...
they will "make it of a sheep".

A o face de oaie.

86.   To Romanians you don't just *"act cheeky"*...
you "take your nose for a stride".

A-și lua nasul la purtare.

87.   Romanians don't just *"laugh"*...
they will "crack up with laughter".

Se sparge de râs.

88.   Romanians don't just *"burst out laughing"*...
they will "inflate from laughing".

Se umflă de râs.

89.   Romanians don't just *"narrowly miss something"*..
they will "miss it by the mustache".

Pierde la mustață.

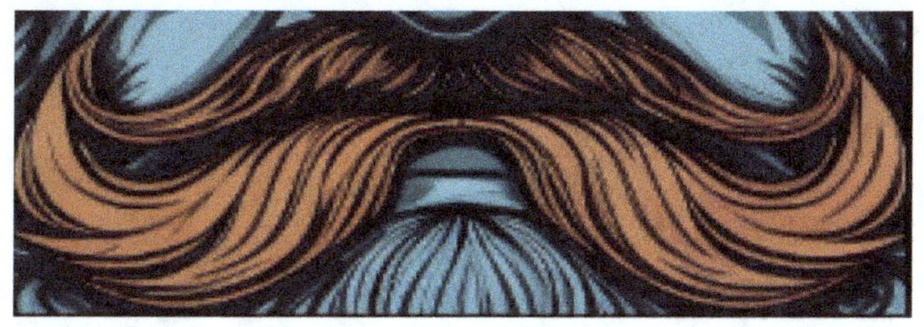

90.   For Romanians there's no such thing as *"it goes without saying"*...
Instead they ask "is there still room for a word?"

Mai încape vorba?

91.   Romanians don't *"drive you mad"*...
they "bring you to despair".

A duce la disperare.

92.   Romanians don't *"manipulate you gently"*...
they "lead you with a little sugar cube".

A duce cu zăhărelul.

93.   Romanians don't *"submit easily"*...
they "put their snout on their paws".

A pune botul pe labe.

94.   Romanians don't *"wander aimlessly"*...
they "walk teleleu".

A umbla teleleu.

95.   Romanians don't *"show off"*...
they "break into figures".

A se rupe în figuri.

96.   Romanians don't *"explain needlessly"*...
they "beat the saddle so the mare understands".

A bate șaua ca să priceapă iapa.

97.   Romanians don't just say *"as if this wasn't enough"*...
they say "a bun over a hoopoe".

Colac peste pupăză.

98.   To Romanians this isn't *"the last thing you needed"*...
this is "a pearl comb for the bold man".

Chelului tichie de mărgăritar.

99.   Romanians don't just *"persist"*...
they go "deep into the white sails".

Până în pânzele albe.

100. Romanians don't just *do something as fast as they can*...
   they do it "in two beats and three movements".

   În doi timpi și trei mișcări.

101. Romanians don't just call something *"worthless"*...
   they say "it is not worth a frozen onion".

   Nu valorează nici cât o ceapă degerată.

102.   Romanians won't call you *"lazy"*...
   they will call you "a let-me-be-so-I-let-you-be kind
   of person".

   Este un lasă-mă să te las.

103.   Romanians don't just say *"how should I know"*...
   they will ask you "Who am I to you? Mafalda? "

   Ce sunt eu Mafalda?

104.   Romanians don't just *"catch you red-handed"*...
they will "catch you with the cat in the bag".

A prinde cu mâța în sac.

105.   Romanians don't just tell you *"to expect the unexpected"*...
they will tell you "no one knows where the rabbit jumps from".

Nu ști de unde sare iepurele.

106. Romanians won't say "something is far away"...
they'll say "it's where the mute took his mare".

Unde a dus mutu iapa.

107. Romanians won't tell you "you're broke"...
they'll say "you don't even have water to drink".

N-are nici după ce să bea apă.

108. Romanians won't just *"run away from their problems"*...
they will "wash the pot".

A spăla putina.

109. Romanians will not just "talk nonsense"...
They will talk in "dodi".

A vorbi in dodi.

110. Romanians won't just think "something is tasty"...
     Their mouths will be left in water.

A ii lasa gura apă.

123

111. Romanians don't just say *"goodbye and see you
     never"*...
     they say "Hooray, and to the train station!"

Ura și la gară!